Aesop's Fables on Stage

A Collection of Children's Plays

Julie Meighan

First published in 2016 by

JemBooks

Cork,

Ireland

http://drama-in-ecce.com

ISBN: 978-0-9568966-9-8

About the Author

Julie Meighan is a lecturer in Drama in Education at the Cork Institute of Technology. She has taught Drama to all age groups and levels. She is the author of the Amazon bestselling *Drama Start: Drama Activities, Plays and Monologues for Young Children (Ages 3 -8)* ISBN 978-0956896605, *Drama Start Two: Drama Activities and Plays for Children (Ages 9 -12)* ISBN 978-0-9568966-1-2 and *Stage Start: 20 Plays for Children (Ages 3-12)* ISBN 978-0956896629.

Julie Meighan

Table of Contents

About the Author   i

Table of Contents   ii

Introduction   1

About Aesop   2

About Fables   3

Write Your Own Fable   5

Drama Games   6

    Game: Magic Rocks   6

    Game: Octopus   7

    Game: Crossing the Circle   7

    Game: If I could be an Animal...   8

    Game: The Lion's Court   9

    Game: The 10-second Machines   9

    Game: Crows and Cranes   10

    Game: Animals, animals where are you?   11

    Game: Sleeping Lions/Tigers/Cows   11

    Game: Alien, Cow and Tiger   12

    Game: Caterpillar   13

Aesop's Plays   14

    The Lion and the Mouse   14

    The Ants and the Grasshopper   17

    Hare and the Tortoise   20

    The Boy Who Cried Wolf   24

The Town Mouse and the Country Mouse   29

Belling the Cat   34

The Miller, his Son and the Donkey   37

The Fox and the Crow   40

The Cockerel and the Fox   43

The Goatherd and the Wild Goats   46

The Sun and the North Wind   49

The Fox and the Cat   52

The Fox Who Lost His Tail   55

The Cat and the Hen   58

The Peacock and the Crane   60

The Dog and the Bone   62

The Ant and the Dove   65

The Crow and the Pitcher   68

Introduction

This book is a collection of plays that have been adapted from Aesop's most famous fables. They can be used as performance plays, readers theatre or just used to promote reading in groups. Each play is between five and ten minutes long. The plays can be adapted to suit the various needs of the group. The cast list is very flexible – more characters can be added. Characters can be changed or omitted. In addition, the teacher/group leader can assume the role of the storyteller if the children are unable to read or not at the reading level required. Also included in this book is a variety of drama activities. These activities are designed to be fun and enjoyable as well as promoting group cohesion, character development and creativity.

Props/costume/stage directions:

There is a minimal amount of props needed for these plays. Costumes can be very simple. The children can just wear clothes that are the same colour as their animal. They can wear a mask or use some face paint. All suggestions for stage directions are included in brackets and italics.

About Aesop

Aesop was an ancient Greek storyteller who is believed to have lived around 500 B.C. He was a Phrygian slave. He was owned by two different masters before gaining his freedom due to his intelligence. He went from place to place telling his fables to the masses however it is also widely believed that he did not write most of them, he just collected them. Aesop's fables were used to offer advice to their audience. He supposedly met his death by being thrown a cliff at Delphi for being ugly and deformed. Over the centuries Aesop's fables have been rewritten, illustrated and translated into every language in the world.

About Fables

A fable is a short story. Fables typically involve animals with human like qualities. Usually in a fable, the time and the place are unspecified. Often fables illustrate how smaller and weaker characters use their intelligence to defeat the bigger and more powerful characters. There is always a hero, a villain, a character with a weakness and most importantly a moral. A moral is a lifelong lesson.

The most common characters found in fables are:

Rabbit

Fox

Crow

Bear

Rooster

Duck

Pig

Eagle

Hen

Wolf

Monkey

Donkey

Mouse

Rat

Cow

Goose

Lion

Boy

Girl.

There are always good characters and evil characters.

Examples of good characters:

Mouse

Kitten

Bunny

Cow.

Examples of evil characters:

Snake

Lion

Rat

Bear.

Write Your Own Fable

Title:

Characters:
    Hero:
    Villain:
    Character with a weakness:

Setting:

Problem:

Solution:

Trickery:

Moral:

Drama Games

The drama games are clearly set out and the appropriate age group and minimum amount of children needed to participate are listed for each one. The benefits of doing the activity are also stated and detailed instructions are provided.

Game: Magic Rocks

Age: 3 years+

Minimum number of participants: 2

Resources needed: Clear space, a wand (optional).

Benefits: To stimulate children's imagination and creativity.

Instructions: Get each child to find a clear space. They must make sure that they are not touching anyone else. The children crouch down on the floor and make a ball shape with their bodies. The teacher explains that all children are magic rocks and that the teacher is a magic wizard. The teacher waves the magic wand and says: "Magic rocks turn into dinosaurs." All the children turn into dinosaurs and move around the room as dinosaurs. The teacher then says: "Magic rocks turn into magic rocks." The children return to their clear spaces and crouch down on the floor again as quickly as possible. The magic wizard can change the magic rocks into anything they want, for example superheroes, animals, people, household items and so on. **Variation:** The children can take it turns to be the magic wizard.

Game: Octopus

Age: 4 years +

Minimum number of participants: 3

Resources needed: Clear space.

Benefits: This game can be used to work on co-operation and teamwork skills.

Instructions: One child is chosen or volunteers to be the octopus and stands in the middle of the clear space. The rest of the children should line up along one side of the space. When the octopus shouts out "Octopus!" the other children have to run past the octopus and try to reach the other side without being caught. Children that are caught become part of the octopus's arms. They are not allowed to let go of each other's hands. Only the children at the ends of the octopus's arms can catch people. As the game progresses, the octopus becomes longer and longer. The game becomes more difficult, as more and more children become part of the octopus's arms. It ends when all the children are caught.

Game: Crossing the Circle

Age: 5 years+

Minimum number of participants: 6

Resources needed: Clear space.

Benefits: This game can be difficult at first but it an excellent way to get the children to use their imagination and creativity.

Instructions: All the children stand in a circle and the teacher gives them a number, 1, 2 or 3. The teacher then calls out a number, for example "3". Everyone in the circle who has been given number 3 must cross the circle and swap places with someone else who has the same number. Once the children have got used to crossing the circle, the teacher calls out a number and a way of moving, such as walking, running, hopping, crawling, twirling, dancing, slow motion, zig-zag and so on. Variation: This activity can also be used for older children. The children can cross the circle in a role. For example, the teacher calls out a number and a character, such as a ballerina, an artist, a lion, a model, an astronaut, a duck, someone who is stuck in mud, a toddler who has just begun to walk, someone walking on hot sand or someone splashing in puddles.

Game: If I could be an Animal...

Age: 3 years +

Minimum number of participants: 2

Resources needed: Clear space.

Benefits: This game stimulates creativity. It helps the children to move and to get into different roles.

Instructions: Each child in the circle takes it in turn to say for example: "Hi, my name is Anna and if I could be any animal, I would be a zebra because..." The children should be encouraged to come up with unusual animals. They could also comment on and respond to the other children's choices of animals. At the end, the teacher could get the children to imagine that they are in the zoo and then they walk around the clear space pretending to be their chosen animal.

Game: The Lion's Court

Age: 5 years +

Minimum number of participants: 5

Resources needed: Clear space.

Benefits: This engaging game works very well as a role playing activity as the children take on the roles of the different animals.

Instructions: Before starting this game it is a good idea for the teacher to talk about the different animals that are found in the jungle. The teacher should ask the children who is the King of the Jungle? The teacher then assumes the role of a lion who is the King of the Jungle. It would be a good idea to have a crown for the lion. The children can make a court for the lion with chairs and a table or with cushions. Inside the court the lion sits on a throne. Each child chooses an animal they would like to pretend to be. The lion tells the other animals he is looking for animals to join his court. One by one he calls all the animals to him and asks them why he should let them join his court. The child must say what type of animal they are and what good qualities they have and how they will be useful to the lion, the King of the Jungle. When they have finished the King says "you may join my court" and lets them in. This is why it is a good idea to designated area in the space that represents the court. Everyone is invited to join his court and there is an animal parade at the end.

Game: The 10-second Machines

Age: 5 years +

Minimum number of participants: 5

Resources needed: Clear space

Benefits: This a lively game which aim at getting children to work together in small groups and use their imagination.

Instructions: Divide the class into groups of five. The leader calls out a machine and the group has 10 seconds to make that object, using their five bodies. Each child in the group has to be part of the machine.

Examples of machines:

- dishwasher
- television
- radio
- fridge
- car
- tractor
- train
- photocopier
- computer

Game: Crows and Cranes

Age: 5 years +

Minimum number of participants: 10

Resources needed: Clear space.

Benefits: This can also be a very useful listening game.

Instructions: Divide the children into two groups. One group is called crows and the other is called the cranes. When the teacher shouts out "crows" all the crows have to chase the cranes. If a crane is caught he/she becomes a crow. When the teacher shouts out "cranes" all the cranes must catch the crows. The game ends when either the crows have captured all the cranes or vice versa.

Game: Animals, animals where are you?

Age: 5 years+

Minimum number of participants: 6

Resources needed: Clear space, pictures of various animals.

Benefits: This is an energetic and chaotic game which is very good for improving children's teamwork skills.

Instructions: Give each child a picture of an animal such as a cat, dog, lion, elephant and so on. There must be at least two pictures of each animal. The children must move around the clear space, making the sound of the animal in their picture. They cannot tell anyone what animal they are. The objective of this game is for the children to listen carefully to all the animal noises and to form a group with the animals who makes the same noise they do.

Game: Sleeping Lions/Tigers/Cows

Age: 3 years+

Minimum number of participants: 3

Resources needed: Clear space.

Other Benefits: This helps children improve their sensory awareness.

Instructions: All the children are lions (tigers, cows or any animal they want to be). They lie down on the floor; eyes closed and stay still, as if they were sleeping. The teacher goes around the room, trying to get the lions to move. If they move, then they have to get up and help the teacher to try to get the other lions to move. They are not allowed to touch the lions, but may move close to them, tell jokes or pull faces. After five minutes, with a loud roar, tell the lions who are still on the floor to wake up.

Game: Alien, Cow and Tiger

Age: 5 years+

Minimum number of participants: 3

Resources needed: Clear space.

Benefits: This game is a fun co-operative game that works very well and is also an excellent listening game.

Instructions: The teacher shows the children the following actions: An alien –the children hold both middle fingers beside their heads and say: "Nanu Nanu." A cow – the children bend forward hold their right hands on their stomachs and say: "Moooo." A tiger – the children push their right hands forward, imitating a claw and roar. When the teacher counts to three, each child must choose to be an alien, a cow or a tiger. The objective of the game is for everyone to do the same action. This will not happen at first but if they work as a team they should manage to be in sync with one another in the end.

Game: Caterpillar

Age: 4 years +

Minimum number of participants: 4

Resources needed: Clear space.

Benefits: This game gets the children to work together but it is also very good for improving co-ordination skills.

Instructions: The children lie on their stomachs, side-to-side, with their arms straight out in front of them. The child on the end begins to roll over the top of the row of bodies until he or she gets to the end. Each child gets an opportunity to roll over the row of bodies until they reach the end.

Aesop's Plays

The Lion and the Mouse

Characters: Three Storytellers, Lion, Mouse, Elephants, Giraffes, Snake/s, Owls. You can have as many elephants, giraffes, snakes and owls as you want.

(Stage Directions: all the animals are in a semi-circle on the stage; they are grouped according to their animal type. Storytellers can be placed on the right or the left of the stage.)

Storyteller 1: One hot day a lion was asleep in a cave. *(Lion is sleeping in the centre of the stage.)*

Storyteller 2: Suddenly a little mouse ran over his paw. *(Mouse comes scampering out quickly and touches the Lion's paw.)*

Storyteller 3: The lion woke up with a loud roar. He grabbed the mouse with his paw and said ... *(Lion wakes up and grabs the mouse.)*

Lion: I'm going to kill you and eat you up. *(Lion roars loudly.)*

Mouse: Squeak, Squeak! Please, Mr. Lion, Please don't eat me. Someday I will help you.

Lion: Ha, Ha, Ha! You, help me! Don't make me laugh, but I'm not that hungry so I will let you go. *(Lion pushes the mouse away.)*

Storyteller 1: The lion laughed and laughed and the mouse ran home.

Storyteller 2: A few days later the lion was out in the jungle.

Lion: I think I will scare my friends. I am very scary because I'm King of the Jungle. *(He goes to each group of animals and roars at them. All the animals are scared and move away from him.)*

Storyteller 3: Suddenly the lion got caught in a trap and said... *(He is in the centre of stage when he falls to his knees.)*

Lion: Oh dear, how will I get out of here? *(Lion looks around the stage desperately.)*

Storyteller 1: After a while he heard some elephants. *(Elephants move from the semi-circle and they circle the lion. They must make sure the audience can see their faces.)*

Lion: Elephants, elephants, please help me.

Elephants: Oh No! We will not help you. *(Elephants trundle off back to the other animals.)*

Storyteller 2: Then a few giraffes passed by. He cried ... *(Giraffes leave the semi-circle and move behind the lion.)*

Lion: Giraffes, Giraffes, please help me. *(Lion looks up at the giraffes.)*

Giraffes: Oh no, we will not help you. *(Giraffes go back to their place in the semi-circle.)*

Storyteller 3: The lion grew cold and hungry *(the lion shivers and rubs his stomach)* and began to think he would never get home to his nice, warm cave. Then he heard the hissing of snakes. *(Snake(s) moves towards the centre of the stage near the lion.)*

Lion: Snakes, snakes, please help me. *(The lion looks up at the snakes.)*

Snakes: Sssssssss, oh no we will not help you, ssssssssssssssss. *(Snakes go back to the semi-circle.)*

Storyteller 1: As night came the lion began to cry.

Lion: Boo hoo, I am stuck in this trap and none of my friends will help me.

Storyteller 2: Then he heard some owls hooting in the trees. *(Owls move centre stage, towards the lion.)*

Lion: Owls, Owls, please help me. *(Lion looks up at the owls.)*

Owls: Tu Whit, Tu Whoo, owls, owls, we will not help youuuuuuuuuuu. *(Owls go back to the semi-circle.)*

Storyteller 3: The lion was very sad. *(Lion starts crying.)* He didn't know what to do. Then he heard the squeaking of a mouse.

Mouse: Squeak, squeak! Why are you crying Mr. Lion? *(Mouse comes from behind the other animals.)*

Lion: I'm stuck in this trap and nobody will help me.

Mouse: I will help you.

Storyteller 1: The mouse began to bite through the rope and at last the lion was free.

Lion: I'm free, I'm free! I never thought you could help me because you are too small.

Storyteller 2: From then on the lion and the mouse were very good friends.

Storyteller 3: The lesson of the story is...

Storyteller 1: ...bigger is not always better!

(Mouse hugs the Lion)

The Ants and the Grasshopper

Characters: Three storytellers, three ants, grasshopper, owls, squirrels and bears.

(Stage Directions: the owls, squirrels and bears are in a large semicircle stage right; storytellers are stage left and the ants are in the centre of the stage.)

Storyteller 1: One hot summer's day ...

Storyteller 2: ... there were some ants working hard.

Storyteller 3: They were collecting food for the winter. *(All the ants are miming digging, pulling and pushing.)*

Ant 1: I am so hot.

Ant 2: Me too!

Ant 3: This is very hard work.

Storyteller 1: They saw a grasshopper listening to some music on his iPod. *(Grasshopper passes by, singing and dancing; the ants stop work and look at him.)*

Storyteller 2: He was dancing ...

Storyteller 3: ... and laughing and enjoying the lovely weather.

Grasshopper: Ants, you are so silly. You need to enjoy the sunshine.

(Ants start working again.)

Ant 1: We are working hard.

Ant 2: We want to have food for the winter. *(Grasshopper keeps dancing.)*

17

Storyteller 1: The grasshopper continued enjoying himself. *(The Ants keep working and move stage right.)*

Storyteller 2: Winter started to come and the weather got colder and colder.

Storyteller 3: The snow began to fall.

Storyteller 1: The grasshopper was cold and hungry. *(Grasshopper rubs his stomach and shivers. He looks at the owls that start to fly around the stage.)*

Grasshopper: I am cold and hungry; perhaps my friends the owls will feed me. Owls! Owls! Will you please feed me?

Owls: *(Owls fly around the grasshopper and stop centre stage. They stand around the grasshopper.)* Twit Tuhooo! Oh no, we will not feed you. *(They fly back to their place in the semicircle.)*

Grasshopper: Oh dear! I know, I will ask my friends the bears to feed me. *(Grasshopper walks towards the bears.)* Bears! Bears! Please feed me. *(Bears are asleep so he wakes them up and they walk to the centre stage.)*

Bears: *(The bears are very angry that they have been woken up.)* Growl! Growl! Oh no, we will not feed you. *(The bears go back to their place in the semicircle.)*

Storyteller 1: Then the grasshopper saw some squirrels. *(The squirrels mime eating nuts stage right.)*

Grasshopper: Squirrels! Squirrels! Please feed me! *(They squirrels walk towards him.)*

Squirrels: Oh no, we will not feed you. *(They hop back to stage right.)*

Storyteller 2: The grasshopper was very cold and hungry. He didn't know what to do. *(Grasshopper is shivering and rubbing his stomach.)*

Storyteller 3: Then he thought of the ants. *(The ants move to the centre of the stage.)*

Grasshopper: Ants! Ants! Please feed me. *(The ants go into a huddle away from the grasshopper.)*

Storyteller 1: The ants thought about it and decided to give him some food. *(All the ants face the grasshopper.)*

Ant 1: You must promise that next year you will work hard in the summer. *(Grasshopper gets down on his hands and knees.)*

Grasshopper: Oh thank you Ants, I promise.

Storyteller 1: That summer the grasshopper kept his promise and worked hard to collect food for the next winter. *(Grasshopper mimes pushing, pulling, carrying and digging with all the ants.)*

Storyteller 2: The lesson of the story is: fail to prepare ...

Storyteller 3: ...prepare to fail.

Hare and the Tortoise

Characters: Three storytellers, hare, tortoise, foxes, badgers, hedgehogs, bears and an eagle.

(Stage Directions: The three storytellers are on the left hand side of the stage and the tortoise is moving around the stage in slow motion.).

Storyteller 1: Once upon a time there lived a tortoise.

Storyteller: 2: He liked to go for a leisurely stroll by the edge of a big forest.

Storyteller 3: One day a hare came bounding up towards him. *(Hare comes running on the stage.)*

Hare: *(He pushes the tortoise out of the way and nearly knocks him over.)* Out of my way you slow coach. You must be so bored because it takes you so long to get anywhere.

Storyteller 1: The tortoise looked up at the hare and said...

Tortoise: I know I could beat you in a race any day.

Hare: You beat me? Don't make me laugh! I am so much faster than you. *(He shows off his muscles and starts to run up and down.)*

Storyteller 2: The hare laughed and laughed

Storyteller 3: Then he met some foxes. *(Foxes enter the centre of the stage.)*

Hare: Foxes, do you think that tortoise could beat me in a race?

Foxes: Oh, no he couldn't. *(Foxes shake their heads in disbelief.)*

Tortoise: Oh yes, I could. *(He nods his head.)*

Storyteller 1: Then some hedgehogs came to see what was happening. *(Hedgehogs enter the centre of the stage.)*

Hare: Hedgehogs, do you think that tortoise could beat me in a race?

Hedgehogs: Oh yes, he could. *(The Hedgehogs nod their heads.)*

Hare: Oh no he couldn't. *(He shakes his head.)*

Storyteller 2: The badgers that were underground heard the arguing and came up to the surface. *(They mime moving to the earth and getting to the surface.)*

Badgers: What's going on here? *(They are annoyed that they have been disturbed by the noise.)*

Hare: The tortoise thinks that he can beat me in a race. What do you think?

Badgers: Oh no, he couldn't. *(Badgers shake their heads.)*

Tortoise: Oh yes, I could. *(He nods his head.)*

Storyteller 3: The bears that were sleeping heard the noise and came trundling along. *(Bears enter the centre stage by making bear noise and taking big loud steps.)*

Bears: What's going on here?

Hare: The silly tortoise thinks he can be beat me in a race. What do you think?

Bears: Oh yes, he could. *(They shake their heads.)*

Storyteller 1: The animals continued to argue about who would win the race. *(All the animals start arguing with one another making lots of noise.)*

Storyteller 2: Then, suddenly the eagle swooped down to where all the animals were. *(Eagle flies gracefully on to the stage.)*

Eagle: *(Eagle uses a whistle to stop the noise.)* What's going on here?

Hare: The silly tortoise thinks he can beat me in a race. Do you think he could beat me?

Eagle: I don't know but there is one way of finding out. Why don't you have a race?

Everyone: What a great idea. *(They all start cheering.)*

Eagle: Right: Hare and Tortoise line up at the starting line. *(The hare and the tortoise start limbering up and they get ready at the start line.)* On your marks, get set, GO!

Storyteller 3: All the animals cheered at the side as the hare ran off very quickly and the tortoise just plodded along.

Storyteller 1: After a while the hare stopped and said...

Hare: *(He wipes his brow.)* I'm already half way through so I think I will have a nap in the warm sunshine. *(The hare starts to make himself comfortable, lies down and starts snoring.)*

Storyteller 2: The hare fell fast asleep and the tortoise walked steadily on and on.

Storyteller 3: The hare woke up suddenly. *(He starts to yawn and stretch.)*

Hare: What a nice sleep. No sign of the tortoise so I better stroll along and finish the race.

Storyteller 1: The hare ran to the finish line.

Storyteller 2: Just as he got there he saw the tortoise crossing the line.

Storyteller 3: All the other animals were cheering and celebrating the tortoise's victory. *(All the other animals start to congratulate the tortoise. The hare stomps off in anger.)*

All storytellers: The lesson of the story is .....

Tortoise: Slow and steady wins the race.

Everyone: *(except the hare who is sulking)* Hip, Hip, Hooray! Hip, Hip, Hooray, Hip, Hip, Hooray!!!!!!!!!!!!!!

The Boy Who Cried Wolf

Cast of Characters: Six storytellers, six sheep, six wolves, six townspeople, shepherd boy, his father.

(The shepherd boy is sitting on a chair centre stage; the sheep are all around him, grazing in the field. Townspeople and boy's father are stage left, miming working, and the wolves are stage right, asleep.)

Storyteller 1: Once upon a time, there was a young shepherd boy.

Storyteller 2: He lived in a lonely valley, next to a great, dark forest.

Storyteller 3: He had to look after his father's sheep and protect them from the wolves that lived in the forest.

Storyteller 4: It was a lonely job, and the boy was bored. (*Boy starts to yawn and stretch.*)

Storyteller 5: He wanted some fun and action.

Storyteller 6: One day ...

Shepherd: Boy, oh boy! I'm so bored! There is nothing to do!

Sheep: Baa! Baa! Baa!

Sheep 1: Why are you so bored?

Sheep 2: Yes, you can play with us.

Sheep 3: We always have fun following each other.

Sheep 4: Don't you like us?

Shepherd Boy: Yes, but I'm bored. I want to be in the village playing with my friends!

Sheep 5: I have an idea if you want some excitement.

Shepherd Boy and other sheep: WHAT?

Sheep 5: Pretend there is a wolf attacking all the sheep.

Sheep 6: Don't listen to him. He *(points to sheep 5)* is always causing trouble.

Shepherd Boy: No, it is a brilliant plan. Let's do it right now. *(Boy goes stage left and shouts.)* Wolf! Wolf! Help! The mean, old wolf is coming.

(His father and townspeople run towards centre stage with shotguns, sticks and shovels as the sheep run off-stage.)

Storyteller 1: His father and the townspeople came rushing to help him.

Father: Where's the wolf?

Townsperson 1: Where did he go?

Townsperson 2: I'll get him.

Townsperson 3: Did you see the wolf?

Townsperson 4: Did he go back to the forest?

Townsperson 5: Has he killed our sheep?

Shepherd Boy: False alarm! False alarm! I thought I saw the wolf, but it must have been a shadow.

Townsperson 6: False alarm. Let's go home.

(Exit father and the townspeople. The sheep return, laughing. The boy sits on his chair laughing and the sheep gather around him.)

Storyteller 2: This excitement pleased the shepherd boy.

Storyteller 3: It made him laugh and clap his hands. *(Boy laughs and claps his hands.)*

Storyteller 4: A few days later, he tried the same trick again.

Storyteller 5: This time the sheep didn't know that it was a trick.

Shepherd Boy: Wolf! Wolf! The mean, old wolf is coming.

(Sheep scatter off-stage. Enter father and townspeople with shotguns, sticks and shovels.)

Father: Good lad! Tell us where the wolf is!

Townspeople: Did he go this way or that way?

Townsperson 1: He won't get far.

Townsperson 2: We could follow his tracks.

Townsperson 3: But there aren't any paw prints.

Townsperson 4: Where's the wolf?

Shepherd Boy: False alarm! False alarm! I thought I saw the wolf. It must have been a shadow again.

Townspeople 5 & 6: False alarm! Let's go home again.

(Townspeople leave and the sheep come back, but this time they are relieved.)

Sheep: YOU FRIGHTENED US.

Shepherd Boy: Hee! Hee! Hee!

Storyteller 6: The boy played the trick several more times. Then one day the shepherd boy thought he saw something big and furry moving in the woods.

(Boy looks towards the wolves but shakes his head and goes to sleep with the sheep. Wolves start slinking towards the centre of the stage.)

Wolf 1: Have you seen this?

Wolf 2: What?

Wolf 3: Lots and lots of sheep.

Wolf 4: Where are they?

Wolf 5: Are you blind?

Wolf 6: Look over there! *(Points to the sheep and the boy who are all asleep.)*

Wolf 4: Oh, yes, now I see them.

Wolf 1: Sssh, be quiet.

Wolf 2: We could have a very good dinner tonight.

Wolf 3: You mean for the rest of week.

Wolf 5: The boy is by himself.

Wolf 6: Yes. No one is there to help him. Quick, let's go.

Shepherd Boy: I thought I saw something, but it is only a shadow. *(Yawns.)* I think I'll have another little nap. *(Wolves come to centre stage and prowl around dramatically, gesturing to the audience to be quiet. Then they grab a sheep each.)*

Wolves: We are mean, old wolves with a bad reputation. It's time to eat a juicy sheep for our dinner.

Sheep: Baa! Baa! Baa!

Storyteller 1: The shepherd boy woke up!

Shepherd Boy: AHHHH. Help! Wolf! Wolf! The mean, old wolves are here!

Storyteller 2: He called and called but no one came. *(His father and townspeople are stage left, miming working.)*

Storyteller 3: They were fed up with his lies.

Storyteller 4: The wolves took all the sheep.

Storyteller 5: The moral of the story is …

Storyteller 6: ... nobody believes a liar, even when they are telling the truth.

The Town Mouse and the Country Mouse

Characters: Town Mouse, Country Mouse, Country Mouse's wife, three trees, three flowers, hedgehog, squirrel, worm, mother, father, child, cat, dog.

(Town Mouse is sitting on the stage. He is looking very bored.)

Storyteller 1: Once upon a time there was mouse called Town Mouse.

Storyteller 2: One day he was bored and he decided to go and visit his friend Country Mouse.

(Town Mouse is in the centre of the stage packing his bag. He puts some cheese in it and then he starts to walk.)

Storyteller 3: Country Mouse was so happy to see him.

(Country Mouse and his wife walk on stage and give Town Mouse a big hug.)

Country Mouse: I'm so happy to see you. Welcome to the country.

Country Mouse's Wife: You have had such a long journey, you must be hungry. Come and sit down and enjoy the feast I've made for you.

(They sit on the ground and the wife gives him some country food.)

Storyteller 1: Town Mouse didn't like the food you get in the country.

Storyteller 2: It was far too plain for him.

(Town Mouse is sitting down, he eats the food but spits it out and makes a face.)

Country Mouse: I must show you around the beautiful countryside.

(The trees and flowers are scattered around the stage.)

Country Mouse: This is my friend the Town Mouse. He has come to visit the country side.

Tree 1: Hello Town Mouse. Welcome to the countryside.

Tree 2: We are very pleased to meet you.

Tree 3: Are you having a good time?

Town Mouse: No, the food is not very nice. In the town you can eat any food you want.

(The two mice continue with their tour of the countryside and meet some flowers.)

Country Mouse: This is my friend the Town Mouse. He has come to visit the countryside.

Flower 1: Hello Town Mouse. Welcome to the countryside.

Flower 2: We are very pleased to meet you.

Flower 3: Are you having a good time?

Town Mouse: No, I'm bored. It is much more exciting in the town.

Storyteller 3: They continue on their way and they meet a hedgehog, squirrel and worm who are all playing together.

Country Mouse: This is my friend the Town Mouse. He has come to visit the countryside.

Hedgehog: Hello Town Mouse. Welcome to the countryside.

Squirrel: We are very pleased to meet you.

Worm: Are you having a good time?

Town Mouse: There is nothing to do here. The town is so much better than the country.

Storyteller 1: He continued boasting about how much better the town was to live in. The country mouse listened very carefully.

(Town Mouse mimes telling Country Mouse about the town. He uses big gestures and Country Mouse listens very carefully.)

Town Mouse: I'm going home now; would you like to come with me?

Country Mouse: Oh, yes please.

Town Mouse: I'll show you things you've never even dreamed of.

Storyteller 2: The Country Mouse packed his bags and said goodbye to his wife.

(Country Mouse hugs his wife and off he goes with the Town Mouse.)

Storyteller 3: The Country Mouse thought the town was amazing. He looked around at all the fabulous buildings and people.

Storyteller 1: When the mice arrived at Town Mouse's house, the family had just finished their dinner.

(A family of three are sitting at a table filled with food.)

Father: Oh, thank you, Mother, for making such a delicious dinner.

Child: It was yummy but I can't eat another bite because I'm so full.

Mother: I'm glad you enjoyed it. Let's go and sit by the fire and relax.

(The family go off to sit by the fire. Town Mouse and Country Mouse start picking up the food.)

Storyteller 2: There were plenty of leftovers on the table.

Town Mouse: There is plenty here, help yourself.

Country Mouse: My friend you were right - the town is so much better than the country. This is the life.

(Cat arrives walking slowly and sniffing the air.)

Cat: What's that smell? *(He sniffs)* I know - that's the smell of little furry mice. Where are they? (*He looks around and then he spots them. He pounces on them. They mice are terrified and start to run.)*

Town Mouse: Quick, follow me.

(They run across the kitchen and into the mouse hole in the wall.)

(The cat yawns, stretches and falls asleep. Town Mouse looks out and sees him asleep.)

Town Mouse: Let's go and finish our dinner.

Country Mouse: I'm scared.

Town Mouse: He is asleep and he won't wake up.

(They creep out slowly and quietly and go back to finishing their food.)

Dog: Woof! Woof! I smell mice. There they are. Woof! Woof.

(A dog enters and chases the mice back into the hole.)

Country Mouse: I'm off. He packs his bag. You may have all the excitement in the town but I'm going back to the country for a quiet life.

(He walks off the stage leaving the Town Mouse by himself.)

Storytellers: The lesson of the story is ... Better to have little and be safe than to have lots and be in danger.

Belling the Cat

Characters: Three storytellers, nine mice, chief mouse, clever mouse and the cat.

Storyteller 1: Once upon a time there was a cat

Storyteller 2: that lived on a farm.

Storyteller 3: His favourite pastime was sleeping and chasing mice.

(Cat is lying in the middle of the stage purring and stretching. He sees some mice and he chases them).

Cat: Run, run as fast as you can. I will catch you one day. I always do.

(The cat goes over to the side of the stage and goes to sleep.)

Storyteller 1: All the mice on the farm had had enough.

Storyteller 2: The chief mouse called an emergency meeting.

Storyteller 3: He wanted to stop the cat chasing and scaring all the mice.

Chief mouse: We must stop the cat. All the mice are frightened.

Mouse 1: Cut his tail off.

Mouse 2: Pull his whiskers out.

Mouse 3: I've a better idea - let's kill him.

(All the mice start nodding their heads and they start shouting.)

Mice: Kill him, kill him.

Chief Mouse: Quiet please. Don't be silly; we can't kill him, or cut his tail off or pull his whiskers out. We need a better plan than that.

Mouse 4: He is too big and strong for us to stand up to him.

Mouse 5: We have to do something. We can't go anywhere on the farm because he creeps up behind us and chases us.

Mouse 6: If only we knew where he was, then he couldn't surprise us.

Storyteller 1: They all shook their heads. *(All the mice shake their heads in despair.)*

Storyteller 2: They didn't know what to do.

Storyteller 3: But then the cleverest mouse in the group put up his hand.

Clever Mouse: I have an idea.

Chief Mouse: Please tell us. *(He gets down on his hands and knees).*

Clever Mouse: Well, *(he pauses)* why don't we wait until the cat is fast asleep and then we can tie a bell around his neck? That way we will hear it every time he is near us.

Mouse 7: That's a genius idea.

Mouse 8: You are so clever, Clever Mouse.

Mouse 9: Let's do it, let's do it.

Chief Mouse: That's a wonderful plan but who amongst us is willing to put the bell around the cat's neck?

Mice: *(individually)* Not I!

Chief Mouse: *(sighs)* Well it was a good idea but we have to think again.

Mice: *(sigh and hang their heads in despair)*

(The cat wakes up and sees all the mice and has a big grin on his face and chases them off the stage.)

Storyteller 1: The lesson of the story

Storyteller 2: just because we say something should be done

Storyteller 3: doing it is often a lot more difficult.

The Miller, his Son and the Donkey

Characters: Three narrators, the miller, the son, a donkey, two travellers, old man, old woman, three children, four villagers.

Narrator 1: Once upon a time there was a miller and his son. They were very poor.

Miller: We have no money so we must go to market today to sell the donkey.

Son: We should get a good price for her.

Donkey: EE AW, EE AW *(stretching and yawning)* I had such a good night sleep. I feel refreshed and ready for the long journey to market.

Narrator 2: The miller and his son decided not to ride the donkey because they knew they would get a better price for her if she didn't look tired.

Narrator 3: They set off on their journey. The donkey walked in front and the miller and his son walked behind her.

(They come across two travellers. The travellers start to point and laugh at them.)

Traveller 1: Why are you walking when you could ride the donkey?

Traveller 2: How silly can you be?

(The travellers continue to laugh and they walk off stage.)

Miller: Maybe the travellers are right. Son, you ride the donkey and I'll walk in front.

Donkey: Jump up on my back and I'll carry you.

Narrator 1: So the son jumped on the donkey's back and they continued on their journey.

Narrator 2: After a while they met an old man and an old woman. They looked at the son and said....

Old Man: Why are you riding the donkey when you are young and strong?

Old Woman: Your poor father is tired and old and has to walk.

Old Man: Get down boy and let your old father ride the donkey.

Narrator 3: The old man and old woman walked off very annoyed.

Son: Maybe the old man is right. Father, you must ride the donkey.

Donkey: Jump up and I'll carry you.

(The miller jumps up on the donkey's back.)

Narrator 1: As they neared the town they saw some children playing in the field.

Child 1: Look at that. *(He points to the miller, his son and the donkey.)*

Child 2: The boy is walking while his father is riding the donkey.

Child 3: You should let the boy join you on the back of the donkey.

Miller: Maybe the children are right. Jump up son and we will ride together.

(They both jump up on the donkey's back.)

Narrator 2: They finally reached the town. The villagers ran out of their houses and began to shout at the miller and his son.

Villager 1: You two should be ashamed of yourselves.

Villager 2: Loading up that poor donkey.

Villager 3: She is tired out. You should get off and carry her.

Son and Miller: We never thought of that. Let's try it.

Narrator 3: They tied the donkey's feet on to a pole and carried her between them.

Narrator 1: Everyone started to laugh.

Narrator 2: The donkey didn't like the villagers laughing at her.

Donkey: I'm so embarrassed because everyone is laughing at me.

Narrator 3: She kicked and kicked.

Narrator 1: She broke the rope and ran off.

Donkey: I'm off.

Narrator 2: The Miller and his son looked for the donkey but they couldn't find her

Miller: Donkey, donkey, come out where ever you are.

Narrator 3: They never found the donkey and they went home with no money, no donkey and feeling very silly.

Narrator 1: The lesson of this story is

Narrator 2: if you try to please everyone you end up pleasing nobody.

The Fox and the Crow

Characters: Three storytellers, fox, crow, mice, dogs, cows, horses. You can have as many mice, dogs, cows and horses as you wish.

Storyteller 1: One day a crow was out searching for some food.

(Crow is flying around the stage looking for food.)

Storyteller 2: She came across a nice piece of cheese.

(She stops as she spots some cheese and she swoops down to get it.)

Storyteller 3: She grabbed the cheese with her beak and said...

Crow: What a lovely piece of cheese! I will keep it all for myself and not share it with anyone.

Storyteller 1: She flew to the top of the tree.

Storyteller 2: After a while some mice came along. They squeaked...

Mice: Squeak, squeak, Crow please share your cheese with us.

Crow: Oh no, I will not share my cheese with you.

Storyteller 3: The mice were sad and hungry so they scampered off looking for food in the woods.

Storyteller 1: Then some dogs came along. They barked ...

Dogs: Woof, woof, Crow please share your cheese with us.

Crow: Oh no, I will not share my cheese with you.

Storyteller 2: The dogs were sad and hungry so they bounded off looking for food in the woods.

Storyteller 3: A few minutes later some cows passed by. They mooed ...

Cows: Moo, moo, Crow please share your cheese with us.

Crow: Oh no, I will not share my cheese with you.

Storyteller 1: The cows were sad and hungry so they walked off looking for food in the woods.

Storyteller 2: Finally, some horses came along. They neighed ...

Horses: Neigh, neigh, Crow please share your cheese with us.

Crow: Oh no, I will not share my cheese with you.

Storyteller 3: The horses were sad and hungry so they galloped off looking for food in the woods.

Storyteller 1: Then along came a fox. He said to himself...

(Fox faces the audience.)

Fox: That cheese looks delicious and it would be perfect for my breakfast.

Storyteller 2: Then he had an idea.

Fox: Good Morning Crow, you beautiful bird.

Crow: I'm not stupid. I know what you want.

Fox: All I want is to hear you sing. You must be queen of all the birds and your voice must be beautiful. I would love to hear you, but maybe I'm wrong. *(The fox turns to leave.)*

Storyteller 3: The crow was very flattered.

Crow: Wait Fox, come back. I'll show you how beautifully I can sing.

Storyteller 1: She opened her mouth and began to caw.

Crow: Caw, Caw, Caw.

Storyteller 2: The cheese fell out of her mouth and onto the ground. The fox picked it up quickly.

Fox: Thanks very much. *(He swallows the cheese and licks his lips.)* Crow, I tricked you.

Storyteller 3: Off the fox went into the woods looking for another breakfast.

Storytellers: The lesson of this story is beware of people who flatter you.

The Cockerel and the Fox

Characters: Three storytellers, the cockerel, the fox, four hens, four foxes.

Storyteller 1: It was a lovely evening and all the hens were enjoying the sun.

(All the hens are moving around the stage. They are clucking and interacting with one another.)

Storyteller 2: They played with each other happily.

Storyteller 3: The cockerel watched over them carefully until it was time to go sleep.

Hen 1: *(yawning)* It is getting late.

Hen 2: *(stretching)* I think we should go to sleep.

Hen 3: Yes, I'm very tired.

Hen 4: Cockerel, we are going to roost but can you make sure the foxes don't come near us during the night?

(All the hens put their heads under their wings and go to sleep.)

Cockerel: Goodnight, sleep well. I will look after you.

Storyteller 1: The cockerel flew up to the highest tree so he could watch over the hens.

Storyteller 2: Not too far away there lived a family of foxes.

Storyteller 3: They were very hungry.

(The foxes come out to the centre of the stage.)

Little Fox 1: *(rubbing his stomach)* I'm so hungry.

Little Fox 2: We haven't eaten all day.

Little Fox 3: We can't go to bed hungry.

Little Fox 4: I want some chicken.

Fox: I have a cunning plan - stay here and I will come back with some delicious hens for your tea.

Storyteller 1: So the fox went off to see the cockerel.

Storyteller 2: The cockerel was just about to go to sleep...

Storyteller 3: ...when he saw the fox trotting towards him.

(The fox sees the hens and starts licking his lips. The hens are fast asleep.)

Fox: Cockerel, have you heard the wonderful news?

Cockerel: What wonderful news?

Fox: There is peace amongst all the animals in the forest. We have agreed never to chase or eat each other. From now on we will all be great friends.

(The hens start to wake up and they huddle up together when they see the fox.)

Storyteller 1: The cockerel was suspicious.

Storyteller 2: He wasn't sure whether he should believe the fox.

Fox: Come down here so we can hug and be friends. This is the happiest day of my life.

Cockerel: If all the animals are at peace, this is also the happiest day of my life as well.

(Cockerel suddenly stops and listens carefully.)

Cockerel: Fox, I hear some dogs in the distance. They must be coming here to celebrate with us.

Storyteller 3: Suddenly the fox started to run.

Cockerel: Where are you going? We are all friends now.

Fox: They might not have heard the good news so I'm not going to stay and find out.

Hens: You are so clever.

Cockerel: I know and now you can sleep soundly.

(The cockerel and hens all go to sleep. The fox goes to the little foxes without any food and they start to cry.)

Storyteller 1: The lesson of the story is:

Storyteller 2: Don't always believe everything you hear.

The Goatherd and the Wild Goats

Characters: Three storytellers, goatherd, three goats, three wild goats.

Storyteller 1: Once upon a time there lived a goatherd.

Storyteller 2: He spent all day taking care of his goats.

Storyteller 3: He would always feed them and make sure they were safe at night.

(Goatherd gathers his goats and mimes feeding them. He rubs them gently and looks at them lovingly.)

Goat 1: We are so lucky, the goatherd is so kind to us.

Goat 2: We would be hungry if he didn't feed us.

Goat 3: And cold if he didn't give us shelter at night.

Storyteller 1: One day while they were out grazing on the hills...

Storyteller 2: ...they came across three wild goats.

Storyteller 3: They were tall and beautiful but they looked very cold and hungry.

(Wild goats come on stage. They look sad. They are shivering and rubbing their stomachs.)

Wild Goat 1: We are very cold.

Wild Goat 2: And very hungry.

Wild Goat 3: It is nearly winter and if we stay here out on the hill we will die.

Goat 1: I know - come with us.

Goat 2: The goatherd will take care of you.

Goat 3: He always gives us food and keeps us safe and warm at night.

Storyteller 1: The goatherd came back to gather his goats. He saw the tall and beautiful wild goats.

(Goatherd mime counting 1, 2, 3, 4, 5, 6.)

Storyteller 2: He had never seen such beautiful goats before and he wanted to keep them.

Storyteller 3: So he came up with a clever plan.

Goatherd: I will feed the wild goats lots of delicious food and keep them warm and safe at night. That way they won't want to leave and they will become part of my flock.

Storyteller 1: The goatherd gave the wild goats delicious food.

(He mimes giving them the food and the wild goats look happy. His own goats don't look pleased.)

Wild Goats: *(eating the food)* Yummy!

Storyteller 2: He gave his own goats very little.

Goats: We are so hungry. *(They lie on the floor as they are too weak to walk.)*

Storyteller 3: Winter came to a close and spring arrived. One day the goatherd came to gather his flock.

Storyteller 1: But the wild goats were not there.

Storyteller 2: They had scampered up the hill. The goatherd saw them and ran after them.

Storyteller 3: When he found them he said....

Goatherd: Is this how you thank me for giving your delicious food and safe place to stay during the cold winter months? You must stay and be part of my flock.

Wild Goat 1: We will never join your flock.

Wild Goat 2: We saw how you treated our friends.

Wild Goat 3: You would treat us the same if someone better came along.

Storyteller 1: The goatherd went back to the goats but they were no longer there.

Storyteller 2: He was sad and began to cry.

Storyteller 3: He wished he had treated them better.

Storytellers: It is not wise to treat your friends badly for the sake of new ones.

The Sun and the North Wind

Characters: Three storytellers, rain, fog, snow, mist, cloud, man.

Storyteller 1: One day all the different types of weather were up in the sky.

(All the weathers are moving and interacting with one another on the stage, then the wind enters.)

Storyteller 2: The wind started to boast to all the other types of weather that he was by far the most powerful of all weathers.

Wind: I'm the strongest weather here and everyone knows it.

Rain: Wind, you are always boasting how strong and powerful you are.

Snow: It is all we ever hear from you.

Fog: Why don't you just prove it once and for all?

Mist: I know - let's have a contest to see who the most powerful weather is.

Wind: I will take any of you on and blow any of you away.

Cloud: Do you see that man wearing a coat over there?

(Man walks on stage.)

All: Yes.

Cloud: Whoever can make him part with his coat is the most powerful. (*All the weathers look unsure except for the wind*).

Storyteller 3: All the weathers seemed unsure that they could beat the wind.

Storyteller 1: The wind was confident he had won even before the contest even started.

Storyteller 2: Then the sun said...

Sun: I will beat all of you in this contest. I will make the man part with his coat.

Wind: (*shakes the sun's hand*) let's settle this once and for all.

Storyteller 3: The wind took a long deep breath.

Storyteller 1: He blew and blew...

Storyteller 2: ...and blew and blew.

Storyteller 3: But the more he blew, the more the man held on to his coat.

Man: Suddenly the wind has got very strong. I must hold on to my coat really tight.

Storyteller 1: No matter how hard the wind blew, he couldn't make the man part with his coat.

Wind: I give up.

Sun: My turn. Everyone watch and learn.

Storyteller 2: The sun started to shine. The sun got hotter and hotter.

Man: What a lovely sunny day it has become. I will take off my coat and sit under that tree over there and get some shade. (*He takes off his coat and sits on it under the tree and enjoys the sun.*)

Storyteller 3: The sun continued to shine.

Sun: I'm the winner. I'm the most powerful weather.

All: Hooray!

(Wind walks off in a huff)

Sun: Gentle persuasion always works best!

The Fox and the Cat

Characters: Three storytellers, four foxes, four cats, four dogs.

Storyteller 1: One day the foxes and the cats were playing in the woods.

Storyteller 2: The foxes were boasting about how clever they were.

Fox 1: We are very clever.

Fox 2: We are ready for any situation we find ourselves in.

Fox 3: We have lots of plans to choose from...

Fox 4: ...if our enemies try to catch us.

Storyteller 3: The cats looked worried.

Cat 1: Oh dear, the foxes are very clever.

Cat 2: We have only one plan.

Cat 3: We might have only one plan but it always works for us.

Cat 4: It is better to have one plan instead of lots of plans to choose from.

(The foxes and the cats are playing with each other on the stage and the dogs come in walking slowly and sniffing.)

Storyteller 1: The foxes and the cats played happily with each other in the woods.

Storyteller 2: The dogs were hunting not so far from where the foxes and the cats were playing.

Storyteller 3: They were sniffing very hard.

Dog 1: (*sniffing*) Do you dogs smell something?

Dog 2: Yes I smell some foxes.

Dog 3: And I smell some cats.

Dog 4: Quick let's get them.

(They are in background sniffing hard and barking. The foxes and cats suddenly stop playing together.)

Foxes: Do you hear something?

Cats: Dogs.

Cat 1: Come on, cats climb this tree.

(All the cats climb the tree)

Cat 2: Foxes, this is our plan.

Cat 3: You better choose one of your plans -

Cat 4: - and be quick the dogs are getting nearer.

Fox 1: Stay calm, foxes. We have lots of plans to choose from.

Fox 2: Quick, let's run behind this bush.

Fox 3: No, we should run down this hole.

Fox 4: The dogs are getting closer. We need to choose.

Fox 1: Jump down this hole.

(They all jump down the hole.)

Fox 2: It is too big the dogs will be able to get in.

Fox 3: Let's jump into the smaller hole.

(Dogs arrive at the hole.)

Dogs: Caught you!

(The dogs drag the foxes off the stage and the cats come down slowly and continue playing.)

Storyteller 1: The lesson of this story is...

Storyteller 2: ...that it is a better to have a good plan...

Storyteller 3: ...than lots of plans you can't choose from.

The Fox Who Lost His Tail

Characters: Three storytellers, the fox who lost his tail, the wise old fox, five foxes, rabbit, two hunters.

Storyteller 1: One day there was a fox who was taking a stroll in the forest.

Storyteller 2: That very same day there were hunters hunting in the forest.

Storyteller 3: They were hoping to catch something nice and juicy to eat.

Hunter 1: This looks like a good spot for a trap.

Hunter 2: Let's put it here and with some luck we might catch something nice for our tea.

Storyteller 1: The hunters set their trap and off they went on their merry way.

Storyteller 2: Along came the fox. He was enjoying his walk.

Fox: What a lovely sunny day for a relaxing stroll in the forest.

Storyteller 1: Suddenly his tail got caught in the trap.

Fox: Oh dear. I'm stuck.

Storyteller 2: He pulled and pulled until finally he was free.

Fox: At last I'm free but look I've lost my tail *(he starts to cry.)*

(Rabbit comes hopping along.)

55

Rabbit: Why are you crying?

Fox: I got caught in this trap and look I lost my tail. *(He shows him.)* All the other foxes will laugh at me.

Rabbit: I've an idea. Tell the other foxes that you are happy you have lost your tail and you think you look so much better without it.

Fox: *(stops crying)* what a great idea.

Storyteller 3: The rabbit left delighted he could help.

Storyteller 1: The next day the fox called a meeting with all the other foxes.

Fox: Roll up, roll up, I have some important news to share with you.

Fox 1: Look at him. He has no tail.

Fox 2: What happened to it?

Fox 3: Did you not hear? He got caught in a trap and lost it.

Fox: I'm here today to tell you that you don't need your tails.

Fox 4: Why ever not?

Fox: When dogs chase you they grab your tails first. If we didn't have them then it would be much harder for them to catch us.

Fox 5: That is very true.

All foxes: *(nods heads in agreement.)*

Fox: When you want to sit down to talk to your friends it gets in the way.

All foxes: Good point.

Wise old fox: You make a very good argument but may I ask you a questions. If you had not lost your tail would you be standing here today telling us to cut ours off?

Fox: *(hangs his head in shame)* Ummm no.

Storyteller 1: The fox hung his head in shame.

Storyteller 2: He left the forest for good.

Storyteller 3: The lesson of the story is misery loves company.

The Cat and the Hen

Characters: Three narrators, a cat, four hens, four mice, the farmer and the farmer's wife.

Narrator 1: Once upon a time there was a cat.

Narrator 2: He spent his days chasing mice.

(Cat comes running on stage chasing some mice. He catches one of them and all the mice look frightened.)

Mouse 1: Please, don't eat me.

Mouse 2: You must be bored with us. All you do all day every day is chase mice and eat them.

Mouse 3: You should look for some other animals to chase and eat.

Cat: Mmmmm perhaps you are right. I am bored.

Mouse 4: There are some really nice juicy hens living on the farm over there. *(He points to the hens.)* Try them. They are far bigger and tastier than us. *(He lets the mouse go and all the mice scamper off.)*

(Hens are clucking around and the cat approaches them very slowly and quietly.)

Cat: The hens look very tasty indeed.

Narrator 3: The cat gets nearer and nearer. He overhears the farmer talking to his wife.

Farmer: One of the hens is very sick.

Wife: The poor thing, we should call the vet.

Farmer: What a very good idea.

(The farmer and his wife go off stage and make a phone call to the vet.)

Narrator 1: The cat listened very carefully and he suddenly got a bright idea. He ran off home.

Narrator 2: A few hours later the cat came back to the farm. But this time he was walking upright and wearing a white coat.

Narrator 3: He walked straight up to the hen house and knocked on the door.

Hen: *(opens door)* Hello, how may I help?

Cat: I'm here to help you. I'm the vet. The farmer rang me and told me one of the hens was ill. May I come in?

(All the other hens come to the door and look at the cat.)

Hen 2: He doesn't look like a vet.

Hen 3: He has whiskers and very sharp teeth.

Hen 4: He looks like a cat and we know that cats can't be trusted at all.

Cat: Of course you can trust me. Now, let me in and I promise I will make you feel better. *(He tries to push the door in but all the hens stop him.)*

Hen 1: I think we will be fine without you. Thanks. (*He slams the door in his face.)*

Narrator 1: The cat took off his coat and said.....

Cat: I suppose I will have to chase mice again.

Narrator 2: The moral of this story is....

Narrator 3: Uninvited guests are most welcome when they are gone.

The Peacock and the Crane

Characters: Three storytellers, the peacock and the crane.

Storyteller 1: Once upon a time there was a beautiful peacock.

Storyteller 2: All she did all day was strut around showing off her beautiful feathers.

Storyteller 3: One day she met a crane. The peacock looked at her with scorn and said...

Peacock: What a funny-looking bird you are. Your feathers are dreary and dull. You must be embarrassed to look like that.

(She opens up her tail and the crane looks in wonder and awe at her beauty.)

Crane: I've never seen such beauty. *(She hangs her head in shame.)* I could never look like this.

Peacock: You will never look like me. My feathers could make a fan fit for a queen.

Crane: You are right, peacock. No one will ever be in awe of my beauty. I'm plain and dull just like my feathers.

Storyteller 1: The peacock strutted around all day showing off her beautiful feathers.

Storyteller 2: The crane just sat and watched her and wished that someday she would possess such beauty.

Peacock: *(yawns)* It's night time. I must get some sleep. It's very tiring being so beautiful.

Storyteller 3: The crane perched herself on a low branch.

Storyteller 1: The crane flew towards her and said....

Crane: Why do you sleep on such a low-lying branch? You would be much safer if you slept on a higher branch like me.

Peacock: I can't fly any higher because my tail is so heavy.

Crane: Have you never flown above the trees and danced with the clouds?

Peacock: No.

Crane: Have you never soared through the sky feeling the wind on your feathers?

Peacock: *(getting annoyed)* No.

Crane: Have you never seen the beauty of the world from above?

Peacock: *(getting very annoyed)* If I want to see beauty I can gaze at my reflection in the water.

Storyteller 2: The peacock walked off in a huff. She was not happy.

Storyteller 3: The crane thought to herself....

Crane: Why was I envious of the peacock? My feathers may be dull and dreary and I may not be beautiful like the peacock but I can fly. The peacock will always be stuck on the ground but I can reach the stars.

Storytellers: The moral of the story is fine feathers don't make a fine bird.

The Dog and the Bone

Characters: Three storytellers, the butcher, the baker, the postman, dog, dog's reflection, rabbit/s, fox/es and squirrel/s.

Storyteller 1: Once upon a time there was a dog.

Storyteller 2: He was always hungry.

Storyteller 3: One day he walked past a butcher's shop and saw a big fat juicy bone.

Dog: Yummy! I would love to eat that big juicy bone.

Storyteller 2: When the butcher turned his back....

Storyteller 3: The dog ran into the shop and grabbed the bone with his paws and away he ran.

Storyteller 1: The butcher saw him out of the corner of his eye and ran after the dog.

Butcher: Stop! Thief! Stop!

Baker: What's going on? What's happened?

Butcher: Oh Baker, the dog stole my bone. Help me chase him and get it back.

Storyteller 2: The butcher and the baker chased the dog.

Butcher/Baker: Stop! Thief! Stop!

Storyteller 3: They ran and ran but they could not catch the dog. Then they met the post man.

Postman: What's going on? What's happened?

Butcher: The dog stole a bone from my shop. Help us catch him.

Storyteller 1: So the postman joined the chase.

Butcher/baker/postman: Stop! Thief! Stop!

Postman: He is getting away - we will never catch him.

Baker: He is too fast.

Butcher: Oh yes, we will.

Storyteller 2: The butcher leapt towards the dog but the dog was too fast and he missed him.

Storyteller 3: The butcher fell on the ground and the baker and postman fell on top of him.

Dog: I'm the fastest dog in the village - they will never catch me.

Storyteller 1: After a while when he knew he was safe, he stopped running and began to chew on his fat, juicy bone.

Storyteller 2: Along came a fox.

Fox: What a tasty bone you have there. Why don't you share it with me? I'm very hungry.

Dog: *(growls)* No.

Storyteller 2: Then a squirrel passed by.

Squirrel: What a tasty bone you have there. Why don't you share it with me? I'm very hungry.

Dog: *(growls)* No!

Storyteller 3: Then some rabbits passed by.

Rabbit: What a tasty bone you have there. Why don't you share it with me? I'm very hungry.

Dog: *(growls)* No!

Storyteller 1: The dog took his bone and continued on his journey. He came to a river which had a small bridge.

Storyteller 2: He walked slowly over the bridge. The dog looked down into the water and saw a dog with a bigger bone than he had. He wanted the bigger bone.

Dog: Give me that bone. *(The bone drop into the river.)*

Dog's reflection: Give me that bone. *(The bone drops into the river.)*

(The dog does actions and the dog's reflection mirrors them.)

Storyteller 3: After a while he realised that the other dog's mouth was empty and he looked like he was going to cry.

Storyteller 1: The dog starts to cry. It was then he realised he was staring at his own reflection.

Dog: I'm a greedy dog.

Storytellers: The moral of the story is we should be satisfied with what we have.

The Ant and the Dove

Characters: Three storytellers, ant, dove, wind, river, twig, two hunters. *(There is an opportunity to have more than one child being the wind or river.)*

Storyteller 1: Once upon a time there was an ant.

Storyteller 2: One day the ant was very thirsty so he decided to go to the river for a long cool drink of water.

Ant: It is so hot today. *(Wipes his brow.)* I must get a long cool drink water from the river.

Storyteller 3: The road to the river was very steep.

Ant: Oh dear, the road is very steep. I must be very careful and take my time. *(Walks very slowly towards the river.)*

Storyteller 1: When he reached the river it was flowing very quickly.

River: Whooosh, Whooosh! *(River moves up and down and gets faster and faster. Blue material can be used to give the impression of flowing water.)*

Storyteller 2: The ant saw a tree. It had a branch hanging over the river.

Storyteller 3: He climbed up the branch and bent over and started to drink the water.

Ant: This tastes so good. *(He drinks the water.)*

(Wind enters. They can be as many children as the wind as needed. They dance around the room making gushing sounds.)

Wind: Look at that little ant. Let's blow him into the river.

Storyteller 1: They wind gushed at the ant.

Storyteller 2: He tried to hold on but failed.

Storyteller 3: Then suddenly he fell into the river. The river was carrying him off to sea.

(Ant bobbing up and own, trying to catch his breath.)

Ant: Help! Help! *(Dove comes flying in and he sees the ant.)*

Dove: Oh look at that poor ant. I must help him.

Storyteller 1: The dove saw a twig on the ground.

Storyteller 2: She swooped down and got it.

Storyteller 3: She threw the twig at the ant.

Twig: Jump on me. I will help you get to the river bank. *(The ant jumps on the twigs back and they swim to the river bank.)*

Ant: *(spluttering)* I nearly drowned. Thank you twig.

Twig: Don't thank me. Thank the dove. If it wasn't for him the river would have surely carried you out to sea.

Storyteller 1: The ant looked up in the sky. He wanted to thank the dove.

Storyteller 2: He couldn't see the dove but then he saw two hunters. They had the dove caught in their bird net.

Hunter 1: Now, we have you we are not going to let you go. *(Dove is struggling and trying to get out of the net.)*

Hunter 2: Stop wiggling.

Hunter 1: We are going to have dove and chips for dinner.

Hunter 2: My favourite. You look delicious.

Twig: Ant, we must help the dove.

Ant: Don't worry Twig. I have a plan.

Storyteller 3: The ant ran over to the hunters.

Storyteller 1: He bit both of them on their legs.

Hunters: AARRGH! *(They drop the net and the dove flies off.)*

Dove: I'm free.

Ant: *(looks up)* I've saved her just liked she saved me.

Storytellers: The lesson of the story is .... one good turn, deserves another.

The Crow and the Pitcher

Characters: Three storytellers, crow, bees, ladybirds, butterflies.

Storyteller 1: One fine morning the crow woke up. He was very hungry.

Storyteller 2: He decided to go looking for some breakfast.

Storyteller 3: Soon, he came across some juicy flies. *(Crow eats the flies.)*

Crow: That was delicious but now I'm really thirsty.

Storyteller 1: The crow flew around and he came across a pitcher.

Storyteller 2: It was full of water.

Crow: At last, I found some water.

Storyteller 3: He pushed his beak into the pitcher.

Storyteller 1: But his beak was too big and he couldn't reach the water.

Crow: Ouch, my poor beak. I'm so thirsty. What will I do now?

Storyteller 2: Soon some bees came buzzing by.

Bees: What's the matter, Crow?

Crow: I'm very thirsty but my beak won't reach the water in the pitcher.

Bees: Why don't you tip the pitcher over and pour it out?

Crow: That won't work because the water will spill everywhere.

Storyteller 1: The crow was very sad.

Storyteller 2: After a while some ladybirds walked by.

Ladybirds: What's the matter, Crow?

Crow: I'm very thirsty but my beak won't reach the water in the pitcher.

Ladybirds: Why don't you break the pitcher with one of these stones? *(They pick up some stones and give the crow the stones.)*

Crow: That won't work because the water will spill everywhere.

Storyteller 3: Soon, some butterflies flew by.

Butterflies: What's the matter, Crow?

Crow: I'm very thirsty but my beak won't reach the water in the pitcher.

Butterflies: Why don't you put these stones into the pitcher and the water level will rise and then you drink it?

Crow: What a good idea. *(He picks up stones and puts them in the pitcher one by one. The butterflies help him.)*

Storyteller 1: Eventually the water rose to the top.

Crow: Now, I can reach the water.

Storyteller 1: The crow drank and drank until he was satisfied.

Storyteller 2: Then she flew off to enjoy the rest of her day.

Storyteller 3: The moral of the story is ....where there is a will, there is a way.

The End

CPSIA information can be obtained
at www.ICGtesting.com
Printed in the USA
BVHW042358190423
662662BV00001B/2